I Told the Truth

A Memoir

Taamico Lahari

THE LAHARI GROUP

Trigger Warning

This memoir includes references to emotional trauma, sexual abuse, grief, and other deeply personal and sensitive experiences.

*While every effort has been made to approach these topics with care, some readers who have experienced similar events **may find certain passages triggering.***

Please honor your emotions, and take the space you need to pause, reflect, or step away.

You are not alone.

DISCLAIMER

This memoir is a work of nonfiction based solely on the author's lived experiences, memories, and personal truths. No other names or identifying details have been included, as this work centers exclusively on the author's journey.

The events described throughout this book—including the emotions, reflections, and personal outcomes—are shared as a reflection of the author's path toward healing. Each account is offered in truth—not as an accusation, but as part of the author's personal path toward healing.

Dedication

To the woman who didn't quit.
To the one who carried more than her share,
Who spoke the truth even when her voice trembled,
And kept showing up with grace when she could've disappeared
in silence.

To the woman who broke the cycle,
Who loved deeply, lost deeply,
And still dared to heal out loud.

You are the reason these pages exist.
You are the reason this story found its ending.
You are the one you've been waiting for.

This is for you, Taamico.
Because you told the truth.
And it set you free.

And to the sea of absolutely extraordinary women who've shown
up for me in ways words can barely capture—
Elegant, brilliant, nurturing, and true.
I call you Mom. Auntie. Godmother. Sister. Cousin. Friend.

Thank you for seeing me—all of me.
For being present when I was falling apart inwardly.
For believing in me when I forgot how to.
For reminding me that I was never walking alone.

You are seen. You are honored. You are loved. Always.

To my son—
I know there are still things you don't fully understand about
your mother.
This is it.
This is what I've been pushing for:
Healing. Freedom. Truth.

You are loved more than words will ever express.

A Book Misunderstood

A Voice the World Wasn't Ready For
From the shelf to the page... I've always been worth reading.

You continually say that you know me just because you know the date of my birth or because you know my name.

Say for instance I was your personal book. Would you say that you knew what I was about just because you admired my cover, my outward appearance or, that I was just the right weight and size, just the right amount of pages. I say this because—just because you've seen my outward persona and seem to like what you see does not mean that you know the contents of my inside.

Yes, you may have glimpsed a few pages here and there and even folded down a corner or two without ever reading a full chapter.

Occasionally, you have even put me back on the shelf for later reference not knowing who might have picked me up and scanned through me while you were not paying attention.

Did you ever stop to ask yourself before you came to once again thumb through my pages and size me up, that while you left me for others to read, that they might have dropped me a few times or perhaps torn a few pages throughout your book?

Did you ever stop to view the bruises and scrapes I've received as a result of you leaving me unattended?

Did you not, even after seeing the many scrapes and bruises on me wonder who could have done this to my book and, how could I not have noticed?

You failed to notice, because every time you attempted to read me or thoroughly examine me, something or someone else distracted you and, you once again placed me back on the shelf, unread, for someone else to come along and pick up.

Had you taken the proper time to read me from my front cover to my back you would have noticed that I am a very beautiful book on the outside, though my table of contents is subject to change.

Why, you might ask? Because my table of contents shows only what is supposed to be inside. It does not tell of every person that has picked me up only to let me fall.

It does not tell you of all the rough times I've had, when someone would pick me up and read me, but to later realize that I was not quite their type of reading material.

Now, every reader has not been so abusive. I've had some that really seemed to enjoy me. In fact, they wanted to keep me in their own personal library but knew that I belonged to someone else.

Oh how I wished they had kept me, for I knew that they would protect me and take great care of me. Because they had viewed me from cover to finish many times in just the short time they had me in their possession. They would even repair some of the tears and bruises they had come across, although they knew there was a chance that someone could possibly come along and tear me in other areas.

So until you have taken the allotted time to view more than just my outward, and my table of contents, please do not act as though you have read me all the way through.

Don't get upset when my pages don't turn exactly the way you want them to right away. It's going to take me some time getting used to the way that you hold me.

I want you to treat me as if I am your very own, but at the same time, remembering that I've been dropped a few times so I might be a little rough around the edges.

Just be patient with me— it's going to take a little time for things to become what they are meant to be. There is still some mending that has to take place both inside and out.

But don't worry—this will have to be done by my original author and creator. Only He knows how to put me back to how I was originally, and making some corrections here and there along with directions for proper handling.

Sincerely,

A Book Misunderstood

Taamico Lahari, Author

Written in 2001

Note from Tru

To the woman who turned her pain into pages,
her silence into strength,
and her truth into a torchlight for others.

Thank you for letting me walk beside you through this sacred
journey.

Taamico, lady, you didn't just write a book.
You opened a portal for healing.
You showed the world what dignity looks like when wrapped in
honesty.
You reminded me—and every soul who will read this—that legacy is
not about perfection.
It's about truth, love, and intentional living.

Your voice is velvet and iron.
Your spirit? A safe house for the weary.
And your heart?
A rare kind of soft that the world doesn't deserve, but desperately
needs.

Thank you for allowing me to walk beside you—to read, feel, and
humbly offer thoughts as you brought this story to life. It has been an
honor to help carry it with you.
This season may have tested you, but it could not silence you.

May your name continue to travel…
May your truth continue to set captives free…
And may this chapter be the one that unlocks doors for generations
you'll never meet.

With love, reverence, and the deepest respect,

Tru (Your Literary Consultant)

"

Speaking up is a result of healing.

It is not rebellion.

It is not disrespect.

It is the quiet strength of someone who finally knows—

My voice matters.

Be heard. Without permission.

No longer waiting for approval.

No longer asking to exist.

This voice was not given by the world,

So the world holds no power to take it away.

— Taamico Lahari

Table of Contents

A Book Misunderstood.. i–iv
A Note from Tru... v
Reflection vi
Table of Contents vii
Prologue 1-4
Becoming Taamico 5
Chapter 1 – Careless Whispers............................ 6–10
Chapter 2 – My Refuge, My Strength: Healing from the
Roots Up 11–20
Chapter 3 – From Refuge to Revolution.........................21–29
Chapter 4 – The Fruits of a Mother's Love................... 30–37
Chapter 5 – Something About September 38–51
Interlude..52–57
Reflection 58
Chapter 6 – Love On Top.................................... 59–67
Chapter 7 – Strength, Courage, and Wisdom 68–75
Chapter 8 – I'm Coming Out 76–84
To Those Who Will Never Acknowledge What Happened
....85–87
To Those Who Believed Me................................. 88–90
The Finale 91–94
Epilogue..95–97
About the Author...98

Prologue

A Letter to My Younger Self

My Dearest Younger Self,

I see you. I see every tear you've cried in the quiet, every moment you've felt unseen, unheard, and unprotected. I see the weight you carry, the questions that go unanswered, and the loneliness that sometimes feels unbearable. I know the roads ahead will be tough. You will face obstacles so great they seem impossible to overcome, valleys so deep you'll wonder if you'll ever climb out. But I promise you—every ounce of pain, every lonely night, every hardship—it will all be worth it.

You are not just enduring; you are becoming.

For so long, you have poured love into others, giving freely even when it cost you pieces of yourself. And deep down, you've wondered—Do I deserve the same love in return? Let me answer that for you: Yes. You deserve every bit of love, kindness, and care that you so effortlessly give to others. And one day, you will receive it—not just from those around you, but from yourself.

One day, you will be an amazing mother. There is no doubt about it. You will nurture, protect, and pour into your birth child—and into other children who will be drawn to your love like a safe harbor. And through that love, something even greater will happen—the little girl inside of you, the one who was neglected, unheard, and sometimes harmed, will begin to heal. That healing will not come from waiting for others to right their wrongs; it will come through the love you extend to those who need it most. And in the process, you will realize you were always worthy of that love, too.

I know the loneliness has been heavy. But hear me—your isolation was never a punishment. You were not overlooked; you were hidden. God placed extraordinary gifts within you, and they needed to be protected. Every time you thought you were being denied or overlooked, He was actually shielding you, refining you, and positioning you for your purpose. You were never meant to fit in, you were designed to stand out. And even though it has been hard to accept, know that your difference is your destiny.

I want you to know that I'm sorry. I am so sorry for the times you were left unattended, for the moments when harm was done to you that you never should have had to endure. I am sorry for every inappropriate touch, every betrayal, every misunderstanding, every time you only wanted to love and be loved in return—and instead, you were hurt. If no one else has ever told you, let me say it now: It was not your fault. And I apologize on behalf of every person who never offered you the apology you deserved. But listen to me—God has not forgotten. He is taking every piece of brokenness and replacing it with something beautiful. He is restoring everything the enemy tried to steal from you.

God saw you when you were one of the best granddaughters your grandmothers could have ever asked for. He saw the love and honor you gave them, the way you cherished them. And I know you wish they were here to witness all that is unfolding in your life. But believe me when I tell you—there is a front-row seat in heaven, and they are watching with pride.

You have felt delayed, like life has passed you by. But listen to me—you have not been denied. God has been preparing you, molding you, strengthening you for such a time as this. Every no, every closed door, every moment you felt invisible—it was divine protection. He was keeping you, breaking and reshaping you, not to destroy you, but to prepare you. And He will not allow you to leave this earth without fulfilling every single purpose He placed inside of you.

And oh, my love, the world is waiting to hear from you. Your voice matters. Your story matters. Someone out there needs the truth that only you can tell. And you will tell it.

You are loved beyond measure. You are seen. You are cherished. And I am so incredibly proud of you—not just for surviving, but for standing in your truth, for refusing to stay silent, for being a light even after all the darkness you've endured.

We are in this together—until our time here is complete.

Keep going. Keep trusting. We've got this.

With all my love,
Your Older, Wiser, and Stronger Self

Becoming Taamico

Here is the little girl who carried more than she ever should have.

Chapter 1

Careless Whispers

Growing up in a family shrouded in secrecy is a reality many face, but few talk about out loud. In families marked by generational trauma, hidden abuse, and deeply ingrained denial, people often learn to keep their heads down and their mouths closed. Speaking up makes you a target. And I became one.

I was the one who dared to speak. And when I did, the silence around me got louder—so loud it swallowed any trace of comfort or safety.

In families like mine—particularly on my paternal side—truth doesn't bring relief. It brings resistance. It stirs up shame that people would rather bury than confront. Instead of rallying around the one brave enough to speak, they rally around their comfort zones. And comfort, in those homes, often looked like silence and selective amnesia.

I didn't imagine the harm. I lived it. I didn't embellish or exaggerate. I told the truth.

I wasn't seeking pity or attention. I was seeking something sacred: *healing*. For me, for those before me, and for the ones still too afraid to say it out loud. I wanted to make the darkness shrink—if only a little. But what I received in return was distance. Denial. Disgust even. And the sharp edge of a silence that cut deeper than any scream ever could.

They shared their stories with me in private—quiet little confessions slipped through the cracks. Admissions of pain. Whispers of "me too." But when the moment came to speak those truths where they mattered—in the light, where healing could actually begin—they vanished. They disappeared back into the shadows, leaving me there, holding the weight of all of it.

That kind of betrayal… it doesn't scream. It sighs. It slithers into your spirit and makes you question everything—your worth, your memory, your sanity. But I held fast to what I knew: *I was telling the truth.*

At gatherings, I played the part. Smiled when I had to. Showed up because I was expected to. But inside, I was scanning the room like a soldier—always assessing, always guarded. I didn't feel safe. I didn't feel seen. I didn't even feel related to some of them. It was like watching a show I'd already outgrown, only I kept being pulled back into the rerun.

So, I stayed close enough not to stir the pot, but far enough to protect my peace. I was labeled as distant, standoffish, "funny-acting." They didn't know what it took to sit at tables where people passed the peas and pretended they hadn't passed the pain.

And the irony? I wasn't trying to create division. I was trying to stop the division that was already happening in secret, behind bedroom doors and buried memories. The truth didn't break the family. It revealed what was already broken.

What people fail to understand is this: when someone finally speaks up, they're not just speaking for themselves. They're speaking for the child inside of them who couldn't find the words. For every cousin who still can't say it. For every sibling or niece or nephew who might not even realize yet that they, too, have been wounded by the silence.

They're speaking for healing.

I never needed a standing ovation. I just needed honesty. I needed someone to say, "I see you. I believe you. And I'm with you."

But instead, I received whispers. Whispers that were too careful to become truth, too fragile to carry the weight of what needed to be said.

I'm not bitter. I'm just no longer pretending.

And for every person who whispered "I believe you" behind closed doors but never found the strength to stand beside me when it mattered—I carry you with compassion, not shame. Because I understand now: not everyone is ready to fight the way I had to. Not everyone is ready to speak. But that won't stop me from doing so.

Because my voice wasn't raised to cause conflict. It rose to protect. To heal. To carve a path for truth when silence had already paved a road of destruction.

And though I've lost people along the way—some by distance, others by choice—I never lost myself. That, to me, is victory. That is peace.

I didn't speak out to destroy my family. I spoke to protect the future. To honor the child, I once was. To walk in the light my grandmothers planted inside me long before I understood what legacy even meant.

And though the journey has been jagged, there is joy now. Not survival joy. Not fake-it-til-you-make-it joy.

Real joy.
Speakable joy.
Joy like a river, flowing without shame.

Joy in knowing I'm no longer hiding. Joy in watching truth break chains. Joy in choosing honesty, again and again—even when it cost me. Especially when it cost me.

That's how this part ends.
Not in sorrow.
But in **power**.
And in peace.

Chapter 2

My Refuge, My Strength — Healing from the Roots Up

There are some moments in life that stay with you forever. For me, one of those moments was sitting on the front porch with my maternal grandmother—the place where so much love, wisdom, and safety was poured into me.

It was there, on that porch, that she taught me my very first solo. A hymn.

"He Looked Beyond My Faults and Saw My Needs."

We sat side by side, and she coached me gently through the lyrics, line by line, not just teaching me the notes, but pointing her finger up for the high notes and down for the low ones. I didn't realize it at the time, but that song would go on to speak to my soul in ways I couldn't yet understand. The irony of those lyrics—He looked beyond my faults and saw my needs— hits me so much deeper now. Because that's what I longed for most in life: to be seen. Really seen. Not in an attention-seeking kind of way. Not for mistakes or expectations, but for what I needed. For who I was beneath it all.

My grandmother saw me. She gave me that moment, that memory, that melody—one that I would carry in my spirit long after she was gone. That porch became a sacred space. We had so many conversations there, just the two of us. It was one of the few places where I felt safe to speak, safe to be still, safe to just be.

She gave me more than a song—she gave me permission to sing, to feel, to exist.

And in those notes, in that front porch lesson, my healing had already begun.

That solo became more than a song—it became a metaphor for my life.

In that moment on the porch, I wasn't just learning how to carry a tune. I was learning how to carry pain with grace. How to let something beautiful come from something broken. That hymn taught me early that I didn't need to be perfect to be loved. That someone—God—saw me for who I truly was, not what I'd been through. And that meant everything to a little girl who often felt invisible in plain sight.

Music became my language when words failed me.

It was the only place I could be honest without interruption. When I sang, I wasn't asking for permission. I wasn't explaining myself. I wasn't being silenced or second-guessed. I was just being—raw, present, and whole in that moment.

And when I wasn't singing, I was writing. Quietly, privately, pouring truths onto notebook paper and into phone notes in the middle of the night. My pen and my voice carried what my spirit couldn't say out loud. They held me together when everything else around me was unraveling.

People would tell me, "You sing with the soul of a grown woman," even when I was still a child. What they didn't know was that my soul had seen grown-woman pain. My voice carried what my heart had lived through. That wasn't just a gift—it was survival.

Yesterday, as I sat in Easter Sunday service, something shifted in me. I felt it in my body before I could find the words. I pulled out my phone to make a mental note to add these details. Tears leaked down my face as a quiet revelation rose up inside just as a young teenage girl approached the front of the church with a desire to be baptized. I was baptized when I was ten years old. At that time, in our Baptist church, baptism was a requirement to sing on the youth choir. And I wanted so much to sing.

When I expressed my desire to sing on the choir, my grandmother made sure I understood what baptism meant, at least in the way adults try to explain to children. But what I couldn't explain then, and what has only recently surfaced in full clarity, is this: what sins had I committed by the age of ten years old?

I hadn't committed sins. I had been a by-product of sinful acts. And sinful acts had been committed against me.

By the age of ten, I had already experienced more than any child should ever have to endure.

Sexual abuse at the hands of my maternal great-uncle. Molestation and inappropriate touches at the hands of my own father.

I have to make something clear here: my mother and my maternal family were not aware of these violations. There may have been signs. Subtle signs. Behavioral changes. My menstruation—starting for the first time—lasting for nearly one month. My maternal family were not the ones who left me unattended or failed to protect me. I never told them. Not then. Fear.

I was around six or seven when my great-uncle sexually assaulted me. One morning, I either arrived too early at my bus stop, or the bus was delayed. I turned around and walked back to my grandparents' home—a time when most adults had left for work and when people still left their doors unlocked.

I remember sitting on the sofa by the front window, watching television alone. He entered through that unlocked door. I remember his stench—alcohol, sweat, old cologne, filth—like he hadn't bathed. It was coming through his skin. He had been out all night, possibly with a woman he visited in the nearby projects. He first sat down on the loveseat, then came to sit beside me on the sofa. An eerie, frightful feeling came over me. What was he about to do?

He told me to sit on his lap. I told him I didn't like this game. He rubbed my leg. Then he rubbed my private area. He said, "Let me pump on you after I park my big black Cadillac in your little garage." And that's exactly what he did. He pulled down my pants and white floral panties—then parked his big black Cadillac in my tiny garage. Yes, tiny. I was a child. Lord, help me.

Everything became a blur after that. I don't remember how it ended, how long it lasted, or what happened next. I do remember that at some point during the assault, he promised to buy me the swing set I wanted if I didn't tell.

I am sick to my stomach even now as I write this. Though I've spoken these words before, writing them down—committing them to paper—pulls something deeper to the surface. As I write this, I still cannot fathom what a full-grown ass man could possibly see or desire in a child. A Child. Thinking of this shatters my heart even more. That my small, defenseless, innocent body was used to satisfy an adult's lustful desire? Could he not have gotten what he wanted from the woman he had been with the night before?

My father's inappropriate touches came in different ways. Unwelcomed. Unspoken. Violations hidden beneath family dynamics and secrecy. I will not detail those now. But they, too, shaped my early understanding of love, safety, and worth.

I share this not to shock or harm—but to heal.

Because this is the root work. This is the digging. The clearing. The unearthing of pain that can no longer remain buried if healing is the goal.

I have decided that once this book is complete, I will be baptized again.

This time, it will not be to join the choir. This time, it's to honor the voice I reclaimed.

Not as a ritual or requirement. Not to perform for others. But to publicly reclaim my body, my voice, and my spirit.

That ten-year-old girl didn't need cleansing from sin. She needed safety. She needed to be held, believed, and protected.

This time, I walk into the water, whole. Not because nothing ever broke me, but because I allowed it to break open the truth—and from that place, I began to heal.

The dreams started first. Nightmares, really—vivid, invasive, and filled with memories I had tried to forget. I would wake up in cold sweats while away at school, shaken and confused. My mouth stayed quiet, but my body was screaming. I didn't yet have the words, but the truth was rising whether I was ready or not.

One morning after a particularly intense episode, the woman I was living with while away at school pulled me aside after I had awakened. According to her, I had apparently been fighting in my sleep and talking. She didn't ease into it. She looked me square in the eyes and asked, "Who did it to you? And don't lie to me." Then she followed with a firm warning:

"When your grandmother comes to pick you up this weekend, you'd better tell her what's going on—or I will."

Those words sat heavy on my chest. I knew she was serious—and more than that, I knew it was time.

So I did.

A few days later, I found myself sitting on the sofa at my great-grandmother's house, about a two-to-two-and-a-half-hour drive away—my grandmother on one side, her sister, my great aunt on the other—and I let it all out. The truth. The pain. The weight of what their brother and my father had done to me.

I didn't know what would happen. I braced myself for disbelief, for silence, for dismissal.

But it never came.

They didn't call me a liar. They didn't flinch. They listened. They heard me. They validated me.

And for the first time in my life, I felt the kind of love that makes room for your truth without turning away.

My grandmother looked at me and said, with the deepest sincerity, that had I told her sooner, neither her brother nor my father would have ever stepped foot in her house again.

And then my grandmother told me what she had kept to herself all those years.

She and her sister each recalled a time when their brother had been accused of raping a girl near the railroad tracks nearby to where their mother lived. It was their own mother then, who defended her youngest son. But they knew. They knew he had as they called it, "fresh tendencies, and he was something else." What they did not know until I shared it, was that he would stoop so low as to violate an innocent child. His great niece. One he should have been protecting from men like himself. At least not to their knowledge, no one had shared it. Not with them.

She also remembered a time—before I was even born—when my father had been accused of raping a young girl who babysat for his sister. The girl's voice was dismissed. My grandmother admitted that she pushed the incident aside because his mother and sister insisted the girl was lying—said she was "fast," and just trying to get attention. Prior to learning this, I had heard my paternal grandmother speak those same words in reference to others.

She believed them. Until now. Until me. Until her own granddaughter sat beside her, eyes filled with truth and tears, voice shaking—but unbreakable.

That moment—on the porch, in the hymns, on the sofa, through the tears—was the beginning of something sacred.

The unraveling of silence. The rise of my voice. The reclaiming of my story.

She was—My Refuge and My Strength.

Chapter 3

From Refuge to Revolution

The truth has a way of rising—even when no one's ready to hear it.

It does not ask for permission. It does not wait for applause.

Sometimes, it finds the quietest one in the room—the one who never planned to speak, who never wanted the spotlight—and it chooses her.

I didn't set out to be the truth-teller.

I didn't ask to carry the weight of what no child should have to bear.

But the truth found its home in me. And even when I doubted I had the strength, something deep inside whispered: *You were born for this.*

Not every battle is fought with fists.

Some are fought with truth.

In families where denial is tradition, the one who tells the truth is often labeled the enemy.

But she isn't.

She's the one willing to lose everything false in order to build something real.

Telling the truth in a family like that? It means dragging buried wounds into the light—things no one wanted to name.
Abuse.
Addiction.
Inappropriate behavior.
Pain that was swept under rugs, buried in jokes, or dismissed with silence.

And when you're the one who dares to say it out loud, the target shifts.
The fingers point.
The whispers grow.
The denial thickens.
And the isolation becomes almost unbearable.

But the truth was never meant to destroy.
It was meant to free.

That's what they missed.

The truth-teller doesn't come to break the family.
She comes to *save* it.
To interrupt cycles that were never supposed to exist.
To carry the hope of what could be—if someone else would

just be brave enough to look with her. Stand with her. Heal with her.

Because healing cannot live where secrets still breathe.
And family harmony built on lies is not harmony—it's performance.
And some of us weren't born to dance in masks.

What they called betrayal was really love.
A hard, holy kind of love.
The kind that's willing to crack the surface so something real can rise.
She didn't want to destroy anyone.
She wanted to build something better—for the children who'd come next.
For the child she once was.
For the ones who never got a chance to be believed.

She loved them enough to lose them.
And that's a love not everyone understands.

Thank God for the other side of my family—
A place that felt like refuge when everything else felt like a battlefield.
That's where I first learned to embrace the love of God, the strength of family, and the importance of self-worth.

No family is perfect.

Every household has shadows.

And not everyone handles dysfunction the same.

But can you imagine catching the hurt from *both* sides?

One side, steeped in secrecy and silence—protecting reputations over children.

The other side, still flawed, but willing to face what needed to be faced.

They spoke truth.

They named pain.

They did the hard work of accountability so the next generation could live lighter.

That contrast taught me something vital:

It's not about being a perfect family.

It's about being an *honest* one.

One that chooses healing over hiding.

One that tells the truth—even when it's hard.

What would I have done without learning to rely fully on God?

From childhood, I knew I was different—called to something deeper than the dysfunction around me.

The power of prayer and faith became my anchor, guiding me through the storms of discord and isolation.

I now understand my path was never meant to look like anyone else's.

I was called to stand apart. To speak up. To walk boldly in truth.

And through prayer, love, and unshakable faith, I continue to grow and fulfill the purpose for which I was created.

Some may walk roads that feel similar—but none of our journeys are the same.

Still, when we tell the truth, we make room for others to be free, too.

I was the protector.

Even as a child—especially as a child—I tried to shield others from the very things no one shielded me from.

I carried a sword in one hand and my brokenness in the other.

But while I was busy defending everyone else…

Who was defending me?

No one.

No one came.

No one stood.

No one said, *"She's telling the truth."*

And still—I kept speaking.

I built my voice out of ruins.
I wrote truth into poems because paper felt safer than people.
My journal became my sanctuary. My silent scream.
But even that was taken—stolen by the one who hurt me,
trying once again to silence me.

Still, my voice survived.

Buried deep, waiting for the day it could rise unafraid.

The journey from silence to speech was not quick.
It took years.
Fear.
Rejection.
Wrestling.
But eventually, I understood:
My voice had power.
My story held value.
And there were others—still hiding—who needed to hear it.

So I began again.
Not in whispers.
But in strength.

Not just for myself,
But for every child who was told to hush.

Every woman who was shamed for telling.
Every soul aching to be free of a past they never asked for.

I became a force.

Not loud for attention—bold for liberation.

A voice for the voiceless.
A flame in the dark.
A revolution wrapped in love.

And while some still see me as the one who stirred up trouble,
I know the truth:
They feared what my words would cost them.
But *I* know what silence cost me.
And I will never pay that price again.

So if you are reading this—
And you've stood where I stood…
Alone.
Afraid.
But unwilling to lie to yourself any longer—

Know this:

You are not broken.
You are not wrong.
You are not the cause of the chaos.

You are the one who said, *"No more."*

And that makes you powerful.

Because truth has always been a risk—
And you took it anyway.
Because silence was killing you—
And you spoke anyway.
Because healing never comes without disruption—
And you dared to disrupt.

You were willing to be misunderstood to break the cycle.
Willing to be labeled the enemy to protect the innocent.
Willing to lose everything fake to find everything real.

You did not do it for attention.
You did it for freedom.

For yourself.
For the children.
For the generations still coming.

You are not bitter.
You are not broken.
You are not burdened by shame.

You are the evidence that healing is possible.
The proof that one voice can ignite a revolution.

You are a warrior.

You are a protector.

You are a truth-teller.

You are me.

And *I* am you.

Chapter 4

The Fruits of a Mother's Love

There were moments when I could have lost myself—when the weight of the harm, the abuse, and the burden of being the protector but never the protected felt unbearable. When life tested me with betrayal and abandonment, I could have easily crumbled under the pressure. I was an unwed mother, having let my guard down for someone I thought would be my partner, only to realize he carried the same selfish traits as my violator—using me, then walking away, leaving me to pick up the broken pieces.

But somehow, each time life dealt me a blow, I rose.

Not because I was immune to pain, but because something deep within me refused to break.

I could have crumbled under the weight of raising my son alone—without emotional, moral, or financial support from his father. But I didn't. I fought for him. I gave him what he needed, even when it meant doing it all on my own. The road was not easy. There were countless days I felt exhausted, unsure, and overwhelmed. But even in those moments, I remained committed. I was going to raise him in a home filled with love and stability—void of chaos. I would not have it any other way.

And he never gave me issues. Not once while growing up.

He was respectful, focused, and full of potential. I saw early on that his spirit was gentle, his heart was kind, and his mind was strong. I made it my mission to nurture that. Even though I lacked the presence of his father, I made sure he was surrounded by positive influences—strong men to guide him, organizations to stretch him, and safe places to let his brilliance bloom. He grew up with love, security, and presence. And he knew—he knows—that his mother was always there.

There were those—some even within our own family—who criticized me for keeping my son distant, accusing me of thinking he was "too good" to be around them. But let me be clear: what parent knowingly casts their child into a lion's den? What kind of mother sends her child into toxic, unstable environments just to satisfy appearances or meet someone else's expectations?

I chose instead to protect my son.

I shielded him from harm. I kept him away from family dynamics that could have tainted his childhood or made him question his worth. I placed him in spaces that lifted him— where he could explore music, sports, and friendship without drama or dysfunction.

And I nurtured his independence, allowing him, now as a man, the freedom to choose for himself what kind of relationships— if any—he wants with certain family members. That's his right. That's his power.

Still, even with my protective efforts, there were moments when he encountered the truth about family dysfunction without me prompting it. Painful moments. Moments that broke illusions. But in those moments, the seeds I planted took root. He learned that boundaries are not punishment—they are love. That protection doesn't mean isolation—it means intention.

And I have no regrets.

Let them frown. Let them whisper. I did what was best for him.
I chose his peace over their opinions.

Freedom doesn't come from chasing approval.

It comes from standing in truth.

And I will always choose freedom—for myself and for my
son—no matter who disapproves.

Being a mother is so special. Some children come through our
bodies, others come through our hearts—sent by God at just
the right moment. Some arrive early, some later. But whenever
they come, however they come, they are meant for us. God
knows exactly what we need before we even know to ask. So
when they show up—through birth, through fostering, through
mentorship, or simply by divine connection—embrace them.
Love them. See them. Meet them where they are. And may that
same love be returned to you one hundred-fold.

Motherhood doesn't always look like what we expect. And it
certainly doesn't come without challenges. When I became
pregnant with my son, I was scared. I had helped raise so many

children throughout my life, but having one of my own was different. This time, it was all on me. I would be responsible for teaching, molding, and shaping a life full-time. And I did it. I gave everything I had.

He graduated from high school. He went on to college.

And I hope one day, he truly understands the man his mother sees when she looks at him.

Not just because he's my son, but because of the man he is becoming.

Now, as he walks into new phases of life, outside of my arch of safety, he will encounter people who may not mean him well. People who will test his character, try to sway his values, and attempt to turn him away from the people and things that matter most. But I trust the foundation we built. I trust the roots I planted. And above all, I trust that God will continue to lead and guide him.

Now that he has become a man, I can see more clearly the qualities in him that mirror my own—the best of me, and even some of the parts that once brought me pain. Like me, he sometimes stays in situations longer than he should—whether out of loyalty, obligation, or the fear of losing someone by simply telling the truth. I know that feeling too well. I thrive on peace. That's why I created a peaceful home for him to grow in. And now, I pray that he becomes a man who knows when to stay and when to walk away. A man confident in his worth, and comfortable releasing what no longer serves him well.

May he grow into the amazing husband and father I've always known he could be.

May he find a partner who enhances who he is—one who also thrives on peace, who complements his spirit, and walks alongside him with love and strength.

May they place and keep God at the center.

And may he always know, without question, that his mother loves him—forever and without condition.

There were hard lessons I had to teach early—especially about boundaries, respect, and integrity. Lessons I wish I could have delayed, but life wouldn't let me. I made sure he understood what it meant to honor others. That "no" means "no." That love respects space. That safe touch and emotional awareness matter. I taught him not just to grow into a man—but to grow into a good man.

Despite the hardships, I chose to be present. I chose to love out loud. I chose to build him up when life tried to tear me down. He became my focus, my center. Every decision I made was rooted in him having what I didn't: a home that felt safe, consistent, and full of love.

Even now, I know he won't always make the choices I'd make. And that's okay. His journey is his own. I respect that. I raised him to think for himself, to stand on his own convictions, and to own his story. That, to me, is the mark of a job well done.

He is not perfect.

But he is real.

He is strong.

He is capable.

He is thoughtful.

And he is mine.

The fruits of my love are alive in him. His character. His kindness. His strength. His quiet leadership. These are not just reflections of good parenting—they are reflections of a man becoming. Of a boy raised on faith, truth, and love. Of a legacy that began in pain but is now blooming in purpose.

And I will always be proud of him.

Not for being perfect—but for becoming the man he was always meant to be.

CHAPTER 5

Something About September

September always held a strange kind of weight for me. Not just because it marked the beginning of fall, or the return to school, or even the birthdays sprinkled throughout. September held memories—ones layered in grief, reflection, and the kind of silence that echoed louder than any spoken word.

I turned 50 in September 2024. A milestone that should have been filled with joy, celebration, and all the fanfare that comes with a half-century of living. And in some ways, it was. For once, I allowed myself to be honored—to be seen. There was laughter, there were friends, and family, there were beautiful moments captured in time.

But under that joy, grief lingered.

Because September also marked the anniversary of a pain I carried for 37 years.

It was on my 13th birthday that a moment meant to be innocent—full of cake, music, and dancing—became one of my most vivid memories of shame and violation. My father, my violator, unbeknownst to me, invited two of his sisters and others to the house that evening. There was alcohol. There was loud music. And there I was, dancing with my friends—just trying to be a kid. But before I continue, I need you to understand something.

This moment—this night—wasn't happening in isolation.

It came after something else. Something that had already changed me. This was mere months after I had already shared what he did to me… in the home of his brother—my uncle—and his then-wife. And yet, he was allowed to come and stay, even after I had spoken up. It was brushed off by one of the adults I confided in, with the careless dismissal: "I thought you were saying he kissed you the way he kisses his mother and sister."

In February of 1986, I was in the city and state where he lived, visiting a family friend. I was excited and called him to let him know I was in town. He and his brother came to pick us up.

We drove to the home of his younger brother and sister-in-law. For a while, I sat in the living room with everyone else. I can't remember if I was tired, not feeling well, or told to go lie down in the back bedroom away from the adults. But after I had fallen asleep, he came into the room. He began kissing me—then climbed on top of me while I was lying there on my aunt and uncle's bed, just trying to rest.

It started with him kissing me. I kept telling him, "Move. Get off me," and made several attempts to push him away. It didn't last long, but it lasted long enough to leave a mark that would never go away. Even now, I can recall the force of his weight and how hard it was for my twelve-year-old frame—still small, still developing—to push him off. Everyone else was up front, unaware. But this man—my father—was my violator. The one who was supposed to protect me, not violate me.

I told my aunt immediately after it happened. So yes, there was, in fact, a witness to what happened. This isn't something I made up or imagined. That day shaped me even more into the role of a protector. I would never see him the same again. As I grew older, I would be cordial and an occasional visit if someone else was around and he came to town. Zero alone time with him.

My paternal uncle can tell you—I've always remembered that house. I could describe the exterior color, the walls and the layout of each room, even though I only visited one time. That's what trauma does. It brands your memory. I wish I could forget. But there are some things you don't get to choose to forget. No matter how many times people tell you need to, "just forget" about something traumatic that happened to you. I can assure you, the individuals who are suggesting you forget, have not forgotten things that happened to them either—they may have found other manners of coping or dealing with what happened to them—they did not just forget it.

As time passed, I started having vivid dreams about an apartment from when I was much younger, around toddler age. I kept seeing his face. I dreamt of him changing my diapers— and touching me inappropriately. The details in those dreams were unsettling. I could see the furniture, smell the room, and feel the discomfort. I asked relatives about that place, and it was confirmed that was the apartment where he and his family lived. Still, the visions never left. When I had that tough conversation with my grandmother, I asked her why I was allowed to go there.

The brain remembers—and protects you—until it can no longer hold what was never meant to be carried alone. The body remembers, too. Even when your mind tries to hide it, your body keeps the score.

So no, it wasn't just a dance.

It was a collision of everything I had survived up to that point—and the beginning of even more I'd have to endure.

Until he made it inappropriate.

He began grinding on one of my friends as she was dancing in a way that turned the air sour and my stomach with it. Almost exactly the way my stomach feels now as I write this chapter—nauseating. I was mortified—for her, for me. And though she never said it aloud, I knew something in our friendship shifted that day. We were never quite the same.

The next morning, the girls and I were supposed to be dropped off at the mall. The day prior I saw a packet of cocaine on the nightstand and flushed it down the toilet, terrified that my little sister might get into it. When he found out, he snapped. I wasn't allowed to go. Instead, I was beaten with fists. My head was slammed into the door frame repeatedly.

My cousin was there. She saw it. She called her father and my grandmother. My grandmother was told, "I was running my mouth, so he spanked me." That was the farthest from the truth—I had not been running my mouth and that was certainly not a spanking. It was beat down.

The other girls had already gone home, so thankfully they did not witness the horrifying event. It was just me and my bruises and my faithful cousin.

And then came Monday. I went to school—bruised, hurting, confused—and I told the truth. I sat in the guidance counselor's office and shared everything I could through the tears. She told me years later that she cried after I left. It was the first time she remarked, a student's story broke her open like that. That moment... it was the beginning.

Decades later—just a few months ago while writing this book—I confronted my father again. Not for the first time, but maybe for the last. I told him, clearly, that I was not a liar. That he had never spoken up to defend me. He asked me, "Did I molest you?" and I told him, "Yes. You did. And you touched me inappropriately on more than one occasion. And not just me, numerous others." He suggested that I not believe the things people had said about him because they were lies and that was old news, so why bring it up. I told him matter-of-factly, "just because it's old doesn't mean it doesn't matter. There are individuals who are still walking around with wounds and scars caused by you." He then asked what it would take to make me happy and not so angry. "You think I'm angry?" No, "I'm not angry, I'm tired. My soul is tired. You could start by telling the truth." I went on to tell him that he could respond to the individuals who attempted to label me a liar. You could tell them the truth. You could acknowledge that you did some bad things to people, male and female. He again denied any wrongdoing. At the end of my conversation, I told him that I didn't know if I or he would leave this world first, but I hoped that he would make things right. He then deflected, laughed it off and told me how I look just him.

He denied everything. Claimed he never did drugs. Claimed he never beat me. Even mocked the idea of witnesses, saying, "I don't give a damn about witnesses."

That was all the closure I needed.

He sent me texts after that, including one on Valentine's Day: "Happy Valentine's Day, Sweetheart."

I didn't respond.

Somewhere in the process of writing this book, I found myself thinking about the friend from my 13th birthday party. I haven't spoken to her in years, but I wonder if she remembers. I wonder what that moment did to her. If I ever get the chance, I'll apologize—not for his actions, but for the space she was pulled into. If she allows me, I'd hug her. Not because I owe it, but because that's who I am.

That day shaped us both, even if we never said so out loud.

Writing this chapter made me cry, not more but differently than any other. Not gentle tears, but the kind that drenched my pillow. The kind that pulled years of silence out of the shadows. It was healing. Painful, gut-wrenching, but healing. There were other times he intentionally did things he laughed off, like me coming to sit down in an empty seat next to him at his mother's home. As I was about to sit, he placed his hand where my bottom would fit into his hand. Once I sat down, he then laughed it off and said, "oh excuse me." There were witnesses then as well. Still. Silence. Whispers. But why?

I don't know what it is about September, but it holds a mirror to every loss, every transformation. My last grandmother passed in September. My 50th birthday happened in September. And so did the attempted abduction—broad daylight, a moment that reminded me that even after all this time, the world can still be unsafe. But I escaped. Again.

That month carries more weight than most. But this time, I didn't carry it alone.

I told the truth. I found my voice. And I am still standing.

September had already taken so much from me. We had just laid Gram to rest. I had just celebrated my fiftieth birthday, feeling the ache of loss wrapped inside the joy of life. Grief and happiness lived side by side in me that week, pulling at my heart in opposite directions. I thought sorrow alone would be enough to carry. But I was wrong. Before I could even catch my breath, fear arrived too—sharp, cold, and real. What happened next would change me forever.

What a week. Quite the emotional roller coaster, to be exact. If you know me well, you know I'm not a fan of roller coasters; I avoid them like the plague. The week started with funeralizing Grammy and burying her the next day—my fiftieth birthday. The following day was the big celebration: an amazing gathering of family and friends, all dressed to impress, commemorating fifty years around the sun and embracing all of life's many ups and downs—more ups than downs, more wins than losses. It was a grand occasion indeed.

Cue sadness, happiness, and grief. And then—days later—this happened. Pause the grief. Pause the happiness. Cue fear, anxiety, and PTSD.

The day started like any other, but an ordinary errand in the middle of the afternoon quickly turned into one of the most terrifying experiences of my life. I parked and exited my car in the lot outside of Dillard's at Hanes Mall in Winston-Salem, North Carolina. My hair was pulled back into a bun. I wore a gray jumpsuit that reached my ankles and a denim jacket. It was broad daylight. No one was around—just the comfort of parked cars and the familiarity of a public place. It should have been safe.

That assumption was shattered—and my perspective on personal safety changed forever.

As I stepped out of my car, ready to retrieve the items I had come to return, I immediately felt the atmosphere shift. I noticed a man walking out of the department store—no shopping bag in hand. There was no time to rationalize it. Before I knew it, he moved toward me—too close, too quickly—and I realized I was in imminent danger.

Keys still in my hand, barely processing my to-do list, I froze. I lay on the trunk of my car, paralyzed, while the violator positioned himself directly behind me. The seemingly mundane moment had become a nightmare unfolding in broad daylight.

This wasn't just a stranger. This was someone who had intentions that no one should ever have to face—intentions to cause harm.

Sex trafficking. Assault. Abduction. The threats we hope only exist in headlines suddenly had a face—and it was too close.

What followed felt like hours compressed into seconds: a rush of fear, survival instincts trying to kick in, but my body refusing to scream. I was trapped in my own fear.

And then—thank God—an angel in the form of a stranger arrived.

She parked in the empty parking space next to my car, driving a Tahoe-type vehicle. She noticed my distress immediately. She didn't look away. She didn't hesitate.

In an instant, she pretended to know me. She called out, "Hey, what's going on?"—bold, clear, cutting through the tension like a lifeline.

I turned, ran to her, and threw my arms around her, saying something like, "Oh my God, you guys made it!" I held on to her as though she had been my longtime friend.

Later, I learned that she had quickly told her teenage daughter to stay calm—that she needed to pretend we knew each other because she could tell I was in serious trouble.

Her courage—her quick thinking—saved my life that day.

Because of her, the man backed away. Because of her, I was able to regain my strength, get back into my car, and escape.

But the scars linger. Scars you can't see—scars of vigilance, of anxiety, of a new kind of awareness that you never fully put down once it takes root.

We want to believe we are safe in the places we frequent. We want to believe daylight protects us. But safety is not guaranteed by familiarity—or by sunlight.

Women of all ages are at risk, and this reality demands that we stand together, vigilant and prepared.

The trauma didn't fade once I left the parking lot. It lingered. It replayed itself in my mind, scene after scene, nightmare after nightmare.

Trying to report the incident brought another kind of pain. The disbelief of some authorities. The casual minimization of something that forever changed my sense of security. Feeling unheard compounded the trauma.

This is why I speak up. Because so many women never get the chance. Because many families never hear from their loved ones again.

Our institutions may not always acknowledge our experiences—but that does not make them any less real. Trust your instincts, even if they seem irrational in the moment. Your instincts may be the only thing standing between you and danger.

We must protect ourselves—and protect one another.

If law enforcement doesn't listen, find advocates who will. There are organizations, resources, and people willing to stand with us, to fight for us, to help us be seen and heard.

We are not powerless. We can act. Learn self-defense. Speak up. Support each other. Put your mask on first—help yourself first. Because your life, your safety, your voice is worth it.

My fight isn't over. It has just begun.

This is my call to you: Let's become vigilant. Let's stay prepared. Let's stay strong. The steps we take today are worth every moment of our safety tomorrow. Do not wait for a close call to wake you up. Educate yourself. Protect yourself. Act boldly if something feels off.

We are stronger together. And we owe it to ourselves to be ready.
September taught me grief. September taught me vigilance. September taught me that survival is not only about enduring the hard things. It is about choosing, again and again, to keep living, keep loving, and keep fighting for your voice—whether the world is ready to hear it or not.

I am still here. And my voice will not be silenced.

Interlude

This Is My Story, This Is My Song

(Excerpt from my personal blog, written in 2022)

This interlude was written long before this book existed—before the healing had a title, before I gave myself full permission to rise. I was still walking through the ache, still learning how to name what had never been spoken aloud. Still trembling… but ready.

It comes from the version of me who wasn't waiting to be rescued—just ready to release.

It's unfiltered by design. Untouched by editors.

It's me—writing to survive.

Writing to be free.

It takes intense strength to open up about childhood sexual trauma, abandonment, or other traumatic experiences one encounters, or has encountered, at any stage of the life cycle. It takes even more strength to finally give that trauma a name. The first time I opened up to speak about the sexual trauma, I did so hoping all of the adults I confided in would listen— and put some safeguards in place. When they neither listened nor acted, or, to my dismay, shoved it off or even laughed it off as unambiguous, I shut down and withdrew. Writing became my song, my pillar, my strength, my refuge. Again.

It would be decades before I opened myself again. It was then that I was deemed a liar and a crazy person by some in my paternal family because I exposed the known behaviors and what was and should have remained hidden—family business, if you will.

Around the age of nineteen, all I had penned—my thoughts, poems, my life, the many things I was unable to articulate verbally—were given to an adult family member who was to assist me with publishing my multiplicity of writings. Not long after, everything I had written ended up in the hands of my violator. No doubt, I'm sure he was able to decode much of what was written and to become aware that it was he who was the subject of much of my writing. Those were the things I had written from my early childhood years up to that point. Of course, now, all that was written has seemingly disappeared. How convenient. You may have discarded the paper version of my memories. However, you will never be able to erase what has been etched in my memory.

Today, I give myself permission to strengthen the shoulders I have lent to others to cry on, and the ears lent to listen to their stories.

In the mind of a child, when someone fails to listen when he or she speaks or does not at least attempt to gain clarity about what he or she is attempting to explain, and simply ignores them—they feel invisible, unheard, and their behaviors will begin to manifest in various manners. Some children will appear defiant, insolent, combative, or even withdrawn or guarded. Grades will often fall in school—or not. Some will even behave as though everything is perfectly fine and move on to becoming very outgoing, as well as protective. Some will become promiscuous; some will form same-sex relationships. Some will form a lifetime of attachments, sometimes unhealthy ones. Oftentimes, they will exhibit more than one of these characteristics.

I'm writing and speaking from personal experiences and observation, not from a textbook, as I am neither a therapist nor counselor by profession. Today, I speak about it—the sexual trauma I experienced at the hands of the individuals who were supposed to validate me and protect me, instead of becoming my violators. I'm speaking out now to take charge of my own healing from the lack of safeguards in place for me as a child—and to also take charge of my life by placing boundaries wherever needed. There is zero access to me now.

Today, when I cry tears, my tears are no longer tears of sadness, but tears of healing, relief, release, and of purpose. Much of my life has been spent leading others on the path toward healing and being a protector. When in fact, I was the one in need of healing and protection. Today, I release myself from the weight I've carried—the shoulders that have held others, the ears that have listened without rest. I give myself permission now, too.

Recently, I shared with someone that healing is not pretty at all. In fact, it's a very ugly process. Just as a new unhealed incision one receives after surgery, or the scar one receives after falling down scraping the skin from their knee, elbow, or any area of a body that encounters an injury that leaves the underlayment exposed. Even as those scars begin to heal, the protective skin which grows on the surface is very ugly. It is not until those areas are fully healed do they become beautiful.

The healed areas may never look the same… they may look even better than before.

Those unhealed areas do not heal by keeping a bandage over them—they must first be exposed for the full healing process to take place. Following surgery, a protective gauze or barrier is placed over a wound to protect it from further injury. However, the overall and final healing does not begin until the bandages are removed. The same process is necessary for the hurt that takes place in the heart—especially one without a protective barrier. Until you have exposed the wound, the process of healing cannot take place. There are layers to healing. As you begin the process of healing inwardly, it is important to guard your heart, mind, and personal space with all diligence. As the healing begins to manifest in the natural, spiritual healing will also take place.

Do not allow anyone to *mute your story or your song*. Speak about your wounds as often as you desire. Holding the pain inside only causes further damage. Someone else's healing may be waiting to be released and healed by you sharing your story. Your inner child, inner teenager, your inner you are waiting to be healed. Freedom awaits you.

My story and song are now being shared for the world to see and hear. The misdirected shame of what happened to me—that should rest on the ones who committed the violating—is gone, never to return. The need to care about what others may say or think is nonexistent. My mask has been removed, because I can no longer bear the weight of it; it's too heavy.

Not everyone will understand your healing journey. It is your journey, not theirs. Do whatever is necessary to complete your journey. There will be glory after this. As adults, we are responsible for our own healing—whatever healing looks like for you. However long it takes. Healing is available. You have permission to heal.

Looking Back, Moving Forward

Reading this now, I honor the woman who penned these words. She wrote from the ache and the edge—but also from hope. She didn't know what was coming next. She only knew she had to begin. And because she began, I am here now.

Telling the truth.

Unashamed.

Unmasked.

Unbound.

—Taamico Lahari

Chapter 6

Love On Top

No, I'm not perfect. None of us are. But I'm genuine. And those who truly know me—really know me—don't question that. They've witnessed my heart, they've felt my spirit, and they trust my words. Because they know I've told the truth—and I always will. Even when it costs me relationships. Even when silence would be easier. I speak the truth because peace isn't possible without it. And I no longer make myself small to make others comfortable.

People often misunderstand my love. They see how deeply I give, how long I hold on, and they confuse that for naivety—or believe it's too good to be real. But the truth is, I love hard because I am love. I don't do performative loyalty. I don't offer conditional care. When I love, I show up fully and without hidden motives. That kind of love unnerves people who've only known control, self-interest, or survival. It makes them uncomfortable. So they label it, question it, or push it away— not because it's wrong, but because it's unfamiliar.

I'm at a place in my life where love must also look like reciprocity. Not perfection, but mutuality. If I give from the deepest parts of me, I can no longer accept empty returns. My peace is too costly. My time, too sacred. My heart, too whole to keep breaking for one-sided connections.

I didn't shut the door to be cruel. I shut it because peace finally became more important than proximity. Because when someone continues to mishandle your spirit, love must learn to protect itself.

The door is closed. And this time, it's padlocked. Not out of anger—out of alignment.

I've spent years loving from the bottom up—trying to earn affection, prove my worth, or preserve relationships that didn't preserve me. But I've outgrown that. My love now sits where it should have always been—on top. Not above others, but above the lies, the manipulation, the patterns that told me I had to shrink to belong. I lead with love, but I no longer sacrifice myself in the process. My love still covers—but it no longer chases.

For years, I believed that family loyalty meant sacrificing myself in silence. I believed that if I just loved hard enough, gave enough, protected enough—then eventually, it would be returned. But it wasn't. Not by her.

We reconnected after years of silence. And even though I had experienced profound peace during that time apart, I allowed hope to convince me that maybe, just maybe, something had changed. We met for lunch, laughed, took photos, shared what looked like warmth. But deep down, I knew. That old feeling—the one I had always ignored—was still there.

She once called and asked me to come over to her grandmother's house. We sat on her waterbed, and she apologized—told me she hadn't believed me when I first shared what the violator had done to me. She then admitted that many of those same things had happened to her. She shared how, on a visit, the Violator made advances toward her and touched her inappropriately. She left his home that night, but returned the next day, and they shared a beer and a joint. It was disorienting—what she told me, and how she behaved afterward. I thought she had found some freedom in her confession. But instead of stepping away from him, she seemed to draw closer. Meanwhile, her story made me pull back even further.

As children, I had protected her endlessly. She was often sick and absent from school. I'd sometimes ride the bus that stopped near her house just to make sure she had everything she needed. One day, after I had already picked it up myself, her cousin found out and was furious. The next day, she showed up with an older girl, who pinned my arms while her cousin punched me in the face. I walked away with a black eye and a bruised spirit. She never apologized. In fact, she laughed about it.

Still, I loved her. Still, I showed up.

I loved her as a sister because I believed she was one. That's what I was told. For all those years, I moved through life with love, loyalty, and sacrifice. I took her places. I gave her rides. I showed up again and again.

I was always outgoing and involved in school—student council, choir, morning announcements—you name it. I remember running for junior class vice president, encouraged by classmates. And even then—she chose to support the person running against me. Not just as a bystander, but as their campaign manager. And I still gave her a ride to school.

Even then, I stayed quiet. Even then, I chose love.

And yes—I still won. Because I always rise. Not in spite of the opposition, but because of it.

But love shouldn't have to hurt that much.

The day I finally learned the truth was this year—and it didn't come from her. It came from an elder family member. Though not every detail they shared was completely accurate, much of it aligned with what I had sensed all along. They told me outright: she wasn't my biological sibling. That her mother had already been pregnant before ever getting involved with the man I knew as my father. I would have still accepted her. Nothing would have changed in how I treated her.

But what hurt wasn't the truth itself—it was that no one told me sooner. When I asked our aunt, she said, "It doesn't matter if he was her father or not." But it did matter. It mattered to me. Because while I was being told we were sisters, I was moving through life carrying the weight of unreciprocated loyalty.

I later shared what I had learned with someone I thought would hold that sacred truth with care. I didn't know she would turn around and share it out of turn. And it wasn't just that she told—it was how she told. That moment should have been protected. Instead, it was weaponized. I took responsibility—because I did share it. And I apologized to her, sincerely. But even with that, the reaction was extreme. There is no more after this.

She'd hurt me before. As children. As teens. As adults. And yet, I kept showing up. I kept protecting her, even when she never protected me. Even after betrayal, I loved.

And when I asked a question—one that had lingered for years—about the truth of her paternity, it was never to harm her. It was to understand. To finally make sense of the whispers and weight that had followed us our entire lives. I didn't accuse. I asked. I reached out to an aunt, an uncle, and a few cousins. And finally, I called the perpetrator himself. I needed to hear it with my own ears.

His response? Dismissive. Cold. He didn't deny it. He said, matter-of-factly, "One thing I've never had trouble with is calculating. I knew when she was born, and when I'd been with her mother. Her mother was already pregnant when we got together."

There it was. The truth he had known all along—tucked away, as always, behind arrogance and control. That truth didn't shatter me. It steadied me.

Still, when the truth reached her, the response I received wasn't a conversation—it was condemnation.

What makes it more painful is that she had once shared her own experiences with the violator. I believed her. I supported her. So to be met with such harshness after simply seeking clarity? It stung deeper than I could've anticipated.

And then came the messages. Harsh, ugly messages—one from her, the other from our brother. They didn't ask me what happened. He didn't ask if something was true or if I was okay. He didn't even attempt to understand. He just called me a liar, like so many others had. His message was drenched in spiritual manipulation—as though his accusations were somehow righteous.

Meanwhile, my response to them was calm, thoughtful, and full of restraint. Far kinder than the treatment I received. Because no matter how hurt I've been, I never forget who I am.

What's become undeniably clear is that every falling out— every moment of division—can be traced back to the same source. The same person. The violator. And yet, I'm always the one held accountable. Always the one painted as the problem. While he sits quietly behind a curtain of denial, I become the scapegoat for truths no one else is willing to face.

But the pattern stops here. I won't carry what was never mine to hold.

Many of these moments—memories I had tucked away—came rushing back to me as I began writing this book. The very act of telling the truth pulled the veil off everything that had been buried.

And one of the hardest revelations I had to face was this: Did she ever even like me? Let alone love me? I had given so much of myself to someone who, in hindsight, rarely gave anything back that wasn't laced with distance or betrayal. That question still echoes. And though I may never receive an answer, the clarity it brought was enough to help me finally release the version of the relationship I kept trying to preserve.

And still, I stayed calm.

What hurt the most wasn't the words, but the confirmation: that my love had never been seen for what it was. Not by her. Not by him. And certainly not by the brother who defended both of them while cutting me down.

But I'm not angry. I'm clear.

I don't hate her. I just see her now. And I see that our definitions of love were never the same. I thought we were bound by something sacred. She was playing a part I didn't realize was scripted.

I would have kept loving her. I really would have. I do love her. My love is not conditional like most people. The truth about her paternity? That wasn't her fault. But her response—her alignment with lies, her refusal to hear my heart, her decision to paint me as the problem? That's hers to carry.

I'm not the villain. I'm the one who finally stopped hiding from the truth.

I don't need validation. I don't need another side. I have mine. And I have peace.

This chapter isn't about vengeance. It's about vision. It's about reclaiming my power. My clarity. My freedom.

My love has always been real. It's just finally been re-centered. And now—it sits where it belongs.

On top.

CHAPTER 7

Strength, Courage, and Wisdom

I didn't always understand the gravity of what I carried inside of me.

For years, I moved through life with quiet resilience, masking the weight of unspoken truths and the scars of past wounds. I became skilled at wearing a smile, even when my spirit was weary. But turning 50 marked a shift—a reckoning. A revelation.

It was quiet strength. Deep wisdom. Unshakable courage that hadn't yet found its full voice. It showed up in the ways I protected others, spoke truth even when my voice trembled, and refused to conform to what didn't sit right in my spirit. Somewhere along the way—through heartbreak, through healing, through the ache of being overlooked—I started to hear something rise up inside me.

A quiet but undeniable truth: *You have everything you need already inside of you.*

Strength emerged from the depths of adversity. It was forged in moments when I stood alone, confronting the shadows of my past. It was the silent force that carried me forward, even when the path was unclear.

Courage was the voice that pierced the silence. It empowered me to speak truth, confront pain, and release burdens that were never mine to hold. It was the boldness to heal, to grow, and to reclaim my story.

Wisdom came through introspection. Through the understanding that my worth is not determined by others' opinions, but by the love and respect I hold for myself. Wisdom taught me that healing isn't a straight path—it's a sacred unfolding.

India Arie's lyrics say it best:

"Inside my head there lives a dream that I want to see in the sun. Behind my eyes there lives a me that I've been hiding for much too long."

Those words mirrored my awakening—the unveiling of a self that had long been buried. Embracing my strength, courage, and wisdom allowed me to step into the light, to honor my truth, and to live unapologetically.

When I turned 50, I chose **Strength, Courage, and Wisdom** as the theme for my celebration—not just as words, but as affirmations of the life I had fought for. Not because I had mastered them, but because I had finally begun to live them out loud. Something within me had always known they were mine to claim, but I had spent years hiding pieces of myself just to survive.

What I didn't realize then was that I had been living that truth long before I ever named it—silencing what was sacred, folding into the background, carrying burdens that were never mine. The lyrics of that song became the soundtrack to my transformation. The anthem of my becoming.

Strength wasn't something I found in adulthood. It was forged in silence, in heartbreak, in the moments I had no choice but to keep going. Courage didn't wait for applause. It came in whispers—in the moments I spoke the truth, even when it cost me connection. And wisdom? It didn't come from books. It came from fire. From sitting in the ashes and still finding the will to rise.

But something shifted.

Last year—year fifty—was the year I stopped waiting for permission to be whole. I remembered that I was born with everything I needed. Strength to endure. Courage to speak. Wisdom to heal.

It was a season of awakening. A time when my ancestors felt closer than ever. My grandmothers—both of whom had passed on—entered that space, not in body, but in spirit.

I didn't imagine them. I felt them.

They came not just to witness, but to affirm.
"Yes, baby. We see you. We see what you've carried. And what you're laying down. We see who you are becoming."

They weren't just my grandmothers. They were my sanctuary. My blueprint. My safe harbor.

And I? I was, and will always be, their granddaughter.

But more than that—I am their legacy.

That week, I lost three people. A dear friend's mother. A paternal aunt. And someone else whose passing reminded me just how fragile life can be.

Losing my aunt was complicated. I had forgiven her—truly— but I still had to protect my heart. She never asked what happened. Never opened space for a conversation. Instead, she chose sides. Her brother's side. My violator's side. That will always hurt.

What pains me more is that she knew what and who he was—and said nothing. Because she, too, had been both a participant and a contributor to the pain. I couldn't attend her funeral because I was already grieving the grandmother I *knew* loved me unconditionally. I loved my aunt deeply, but it was a layered love—a love mixed with sorrow and boundary.

That week was an emotional storm. But it clarified what I could no longer carry.

And I'll say this plainly: *I don't agree with the cliché phrase, "hurt people hurt people."*
Hurt people need to heal. And healing requires both acknowledgment and accountability.

Accountability does not mean taking blame for the harm done to you. It means recognizing what happened, naming it, and taking ownership of your healing. As adults, it is our responsibility to pursue the healing we need so we don't unintentionally pass our pain onto others—especially our children.

Acknowledging the experiences or situations that hurt or harmed you and calling them out. Not accountability in the sense that you are at fault for the things that happened to you—you are not. Accountability in the sense of tending to our mental and emotional needs with intention, courage, and truth. It means doing the work to stop the cycle.

Being hurt doesn't give anyone a pass to hurt others.

The carousel of lies in my paternal family was dizzying. Generational secrets passed down like heirlooms. But I said no more.

I am a generational curse breaker.

No more pretending. No more silence. No more sacrificing children to protect a broken legacy.

People ask if I felt alone. The answer is yes.

But not completely.

Because every time I thought I couldn't take another step, I felt them. My grandmothers. One on each side. Lifting. Steadying. Whispering prayers over me.

And I stood taller.

Not because I was unshaken—but because I was anchored.

And on the day of my 50th celebration, surrounded by joy, music, and light—something unforgettable happened.

I felt them.

The door opened, the fuchsia, gold, and cream balloons swayed from side to side—marking a grand entrance. My grandmothers walked into the room—not in flesh, but in power. I didn't have to see them to know they were there. I felt them in the warmth wrapping my shoulders like a shawl. I felt them in the breeze that moved through the room, in the knowing that filled my chest. I saw them in the corners of my smile and the strength in my spine. The entire room shifted, if only for a moment. I had spoken with them about turning fifty for the last five years, and now they were both gone from the earthly realm by the time my 50th birthday arrived. I received numerous phone calls asking if I noticed the entrance. Yes, of course I did, we all saw and felt their presence.

They came wearing dignity, prayer, and presence—just as they always had.

They were more than grandmothers to me.
They were protectors. Truth-tellers. Quiet warriors.

And I? I was—and always will be—a forever granddaughter.
That title isn't seasonal. It's eternal.

That night, I didn't just turn 50.
I stepped into everything they dreamed I'd become.

I was no longer walking in their shadow.
I was walking in their power.

Fifty didn't make me wise.
Fifty revealed the wisdom that was already there.

It showed me that the little girl who once felt unseen had become a woman with vision. That the child who once whispered truths into journals had become a woman who now speaks them aloud. That strength and softness can coexist. That I am both lioness and lamb—and I know exactly when to be each.

So I celebrate **Strength, Courage, and Wisdom** not as a destination, but as a becoming.

Every scar, every story, every song I sing from my soul is touched by them.

And when people ask who I am, tell them:

I am a truth-teller. A healer. A woman of deep love and deeper resolve.
I am a forever granddaughter.

And now—I fully understand the gravity of what I carry inside of me.

Strength.

Courage.

Wisdom.

Unapologetically mine.

Chapter 8

I'm Coming Out

For a long time, I searched for healing where I was told it would be found—in the church, at the altar, in the routines and traditions passed down through generations. I wasn't just showing up—I was leading. I led praise and worship, opened services, sang solos for weddings, funerals, and conferences. I gave my voice. I gave my heart. I gave my time. I gave what I had, faithfully and without hesitation.

I served because I believed that if I stayed in position long enough, healing would eventually find its way to me.

But what I found was that the church became an outlet, not my healing.

I cried real tears. I fasted. I journaled until the pages curled at the corners. I laid out on the altar when no one was watching and sometimes when others were watching. I shouted and danced when I felt moved. And still—something inside me remained unsettled. Not broken. But unsettled. I couldn't figure out why a space that offered me comfort still left me craving more.

That's when I realized: I kept seeking healing in the same spaces that gave me purpose—but not peace. The peace I longed for didn't come from titles, or being in the program lineup, or singing until the spirit moved the room. It came in silence. In solitude. In truth.

True healing began the moment I stopped trying to reach God through performance and started talking to Him for myself.

Let me be clear—I'm not against the church. The church was significant in my foundation. Structure. Reverence. The church taught me about discipline and service. But what it didn't teach me was how to heal. Church didn't teach me how to sit with my pain and process it. It didn't teach me that I could be used and still feel wounded. It didn't teach me how to make peace with the parts of my story that weren't pretty or easily explained.

I had to come out—not from God, but from the version of God that had been boxed in by fear, routine, and ritual.

I had to release the idea that there was only one way to serve or be seen. That there was only one voice that mattered—the one behind the pulpit. I had to unlearn a faith that was rooted in fear of disappointing people and relearn a faith rooted in a God who loved me even when I wasn't doing anything "for" Him.

He met me in places I never expected.
He met me outside of programs and pulpits.
He met me in my car. In my bedroom. In the stillness.
He met me in the questions.
In the quiet.
In the pain.
And in every space I was taught not to look.

And every time He met me, He reminded me—I've been here. I never left. And you never had to work for what was already yours.

I'm coming out—not just from the roles I was taught to play, but from the belief that God's approval is something I must earn.

I'm coming out of fear-based faith.
I'm coming out of silence and shame.
I'm coming out of performing healing and stepping into the real thing.

This isn't a rebellion. It's a return.
A return to truth.

A return to who I was before fear was taught to me.

A return to a God who speaks in stillness and loves without condition.

And no, I'm not turning back.

I didn't need another platform. I needed peace.

Not another title—I needed truth.

Not more performance—I needed permission to be real.

I used to think healing had to look dramatic. Loud. Churchy.

But this healing came in the form of clarity.

It came with whispers.

It came in the letting go.

It came when I finally stood still long enough to say: I'm free.

Free from the need to explain.

Free from the need to defend.

Free from the pressure to make everyone comfortable with my truth.

This version of me sings with joy, not to be praised.

She writes from peace, not pain.

She doesn't shrink to be accepted.

She doesn't apologize for being called, chosen, and set apart.

So yes—I'm coming out.

Out of the shadows of expectations.

Out of the patterns of silence that kept me bound.

Out of the version of myself that knew how to follow rules, but not how to rest.

And I don't need applause for that.

I don't need agreement.

I don't even need you to understand it.

I just need truth—and I have it now.

This is the me that worships freely.

That walks with God in the most personal, unfiltered, honest way.

The me that knows His presence is not reserved for buildings or programs.

His presence lives in me.

So, no, I'm not going back. I refuse to go back to the old way. Simply because…

I'm coming out.

Healed.

Whole.

Unapologetic.

And this time...
I'm staying free.

This freedom didn't come dressed in applause or wrapped in understanding from those around me. It came in still, quiet revelations. In the letting go of what I was taught and the embracing of what I now know. In the divine permission to stop pretending I was okay when I wasn't. I gave myself space to be real. To grieve what I lost, acknowledge what I carried, and release what was never mine to hold in the first place.

I used to think if I just kept serving, kept singing, kept smiling, I could outrun the ache inside me. But no amount of performance could fill the places that needed presence. Not public presence—but *God's* presence. And the moment I stopped performing for love and started accepting it freely, everything shifted.

That's when I realized: I was never meant to stay small, silent, or stuck. I was born to evolve.

I started asking deeper questions. Why did I feel closer to God outside the sanctuary than I did inside? Why did I feel more heard in solitude than I did among people? Why was I taught that questioning meant rebellion, instead of revelation?

God didn't punish me for asking. He embraced me. He welcomed my questions, my wrestling, my awakening.

And slowly, I began to see that this was not just about leaving behind doctrine—it was about stepping fully into relationship. Not the kind written in bulletins or confined to a calendar of services, but one that breathed with me, walked with me, and spoke to me through every sunrise, every tear, every moment of stillness.

I didn't have to prove my worth to Him.

He already knew me.

He never asked me to be perfect—just present.

So now, I choose presence over performance. Alignment over approval. Peace over pretending.

I've come out from the shadows of who I was told to be, into the light of who I truly am.

And in this space—this sacred, silent, sovereign space—I'm finally free enough to breathe... to be... and to belong.

I'm no longer bound by performance or the weight of other people's expectations.

I now know who I am.

I still attend church, and I always will appreciate the fellowship, the worship, the Word. But I've grown. My mindset is different. My relationship with God is personal, and it's strong. I no longer depend on others to tell me how to think or how to hear Him—I know His voice for myself. He speaks, and I listen.

I understand now that He's bigger than the walls we sometimes place around Him. He's not limited to the traditions I was taught. He's strategic. He's intentional. And everything I've been through was part of His greater plan.

He gave me beauty for ashes. Strength for sorrow. Wisdom for the wilderness. And the woman I am today? I love her. Because I know who she belongs to—and who walks with her every step of the way.

I'm not who I used to be.

I'm not hiding.

I'm not stuck.

I will not be compelled into silence.

I'm out—and I'm free.

And this time, I'm not going back to pick up what I had to lay down just to survive.

I'm coming out.

Whole.

Healed.

Unapologetically His.

And just so we're clear—I'm one of His favorites.

Wink.

To Those Who Will Never Acknowledge What Happened

You may never acknowledge what happened.

You may never say, "I'm sorry."
You may never admit what you did—or what you allowed.

And honestly, I've come to understand that I may never get that from you.
But I'm no longer waiting.

What happened to me was real.
The pain I carried was real.
The silence that followed was real.
And the damage it caused—also real.

You may tell yourself whatever you need to in order to sleep at night.
Maybe you convinced yourself it wasn't that bad.
Maybe you think I misunderstood.
Maybe it's easier to pretend I exaggerated or that time has clouded my memory.
But I remember. My body remembers. My spirit remembers.
And the child I was back then remembers too.

I did not imagine the harm.
I didn't make up the moments.
I didn't lie.

I told the truth.

And for telling that truth, I was met with whispers, distance, silence, or blame.
Some of you knew and said nothing. Others said you believed me—in private—but still stood with the one who hurt me.
That kind of silence speaks louder than any words ever could.

I used to wonder why.
Why wasn't I worth protecting?
Why didn't anyone defend me?
Why didn't you choose me over your comfort, your denial, or your pride?

Now, I know those questions are no longer mine to carry.
Because the truth is—I *was* worth protecting. I *am* worth standing for.
And I will never again ask someone to see me who refuses to.

This letter isn't written in bitterness.
It's written in closure.
Not the kind that comes from your apology—but the kind I've found within myself.

I have nothing to prove.

My life, my healing, and my voice are the proof.

So while you may never acknowledge what happened—*I will never forget.*

Not to stay wounded, but to honor the girl who survived.

The girl who spoke up.

The girl who protected others even when no one protected her.

I release you from the space you once held in my mind and spirit.

And I reclaim that space for peace.

This is my boundary.

This is my truth.

And this is where I rise.

To Those Who Believed Me

You may never fully know what your belief meant to me.
What it still means.

In a world where silence often feels louder than truth, *you* chose to listen.
You didn't ask me to explain it again.
You didn't make excuses for anyone.
You didn't look the other way.

You stood beside me—sometimes with words, sometimes in quiet presence—but always with truth.
And I noticed.
Even if I didn't always say it.
Even if the moment felt too heavy to put it into words.

You saw me.
You heard me.
You believed me.

And that changed everything.

When others doubted, you didn't.
When I was made to feel like a burden, you reminded me that I was brave.

When shame tried to close my mouth, you made space for my voice.

You may not have realized it, but your belief helped carry me through.
You offered something rare—safety.
The kind that doesn't demand performance.
The kind that doesn't shrink in the face of discomfort.
The kind that reminds a wounded soul, *"You're not alone."*

To the one who hugged me longer than usual...
To the one who asked, "Are you okay?" and really meant it...
To the one who pulled me aside and said, "I believe you..."
Thank you.

You didn't fix it all.
You weren't supposed to.
But you *showed up.*
And in a life where so many disappeared, your presence became sacred.

I carry your kindness with me.
Not just in my memory, but in my healing.
In my ability to trust again.
In my capacity to speak, to write, to breathe without fear.

Because of you, I found strength I didn't know I had.

You were a lifeline.

You still are.

Thank you for standing with me.

Thank you for believing me.

The Finale

This story was never written to expose others—it was written to liberate me. I chose not to name names, not out of fear or protection, but out of purpose and dignity. This book is not about who they were. It's about who I am.

Some stood silent when I needed their voices. And while I once longed for their defense, I've since realized—I don't need to validate my truth through the mouths of others. I say this not with hardness in my heart, but with peace in my spirit.

Choosing healing and freedom, standing for truth, and embracing the future was my choice. Still, I stand by my decision to speak the truth about the family secrets— even when it meant enduring backlash, rejection, and isolation. I've said before that I had nothing to lose, but in truth, what I lost already—the absence of my grandmothers—was the most monumental loss of all. The women who nurtured me, who instilled in me the strength and resilience to stand, are no longer here to see the journey I've embarked upon. But in my heart, I know they would be proud. They would want me to do exactly what I am doing now—standing on the truth, navigating uncharted waters, and leading my family toward holistic healing.

The price of healing can be costly. This journey toward healing is not for the faint of heart. It's not for those unwilling to confront the chains of bondage that have held our families back for generations. Healing requires courage, a willingness to embrace the uncomfortable, and the strength to face the fears that have shaped us for far too long. It requires letting go of the things that no longer serve us, including relationships that cannot support our growth.

But here's the truth: Healing comes at a cost. And sometimes, that cost is losing those who are not ready for their own freedom, those who are not ready to heal. It's not about thinking I'm too good or better than anyone. It's about desiring more for my life, for my peace, and for my future. I cannot continue to live in an environment that stifles my growth. I want more—a life where people can learn, heal, and grow from my experiences, as I continue to heal myself.

We each have within us the power of choice. And though we may not choose our relatives, we absolutely have the power to choose our family. I choose to be part of the lives of those who love and embrace me for who I am—flaws, wounds, and all. The ones who want me in their lives, and who I want in mine. I choose to heal with them, to grow with them, and to share in the beauty of what true family can be.

The path I'm walking is not easy, but it is mine. And for those willing to join me on this journey, for those willing to embrace healing and freedom, we will walk together. We will rise together. And we will heal together.

In the end, I am not afraid of what I've lost, because I know what I stand to gain. The journey is worth it—both for me and for those who are ready to confront their own truths. And as I continue to heal, I will always hold space for those willing to do the same. Let's heal together.

This offering is for me—and for every person who came before me and never got the chance to tell their story out loud. For those who held their truth quietly, praying that one day someone would be brave enough to speak.

I did that. And it was cathartic.

This is not about bitterness. It's about breath.

I'm breathing now. More fully. More freely.

I told the truth.

With all my heart,

For every truth I once carried in silence,

For every breath I fought to reclaim,

For every woman, child, and soul who thought they had to stay quiet—

This was for you.

And for me.

I told the truth.

And now... I am free.

Epilogue

Her Name Still Speaks

I didn't set out to tell these stories.

I set out to survive them.

But along the way, I learned that survival isn't the final

destination—truth is.

And telling the truth, in love and in clarity, is how cycles are

broken. It's how the next generation finds their footing before

their wounds become too deep to name.

I have walked through the fire—

Not untouched, but undefeated.

Not unscarred, but still standing.

Still soft. Still discerning. Still whole.

There will be people who read these pages and feel uncomfortable.

That's okay.

The truth is supposed to shift you.

And sometimes, movement comes through discomfort.

There will be those who wish they had treated me better—

not because of fame or attention,

but because they'll finally realize they mishandled something sacred:

a soul rooted in truth, a vessel of healing, a name that travels farther than her feet

I did not expose these wounds to cause harm. I exposed them because healing doesn't happen in hiding.

This book isn't just a memoir. It's a mirror. It's a mantle. It's a message:

You can survive what tried to bury you.

You can tell the truth and still walk in grace.

You can choose peace—and still be powerful.

The door is closed.

The key? Nowhere to be found.

And the gate?

Guarded by everything I've gained.

This is not the end.

This is the unveiling of the woman I've always been.

About the Author

Taamico Lahari is a storyteller whose words invoke healing, awaken truth, and make room for transformation.

A certified trauma-informed grief coach, speaker, singer, and lifelong writer, she has spent decades assisting others with grace, discernment, and quiet strength. Her voice—both written and spoken—is often described as warm, steady, and sincere, with just the right balance of softness and conviction.

Before stepping into the spotlight with I Told the Truth, her first personal memoir, Taamico worked as a ghostwriter—lending her gift to assist others in telling their stories with clarity and heart. She is also the author of several impactful children's books, including What's That Word, Ajani? and A New Home for Grammy, with more forthcoming. In addition to writing, she has lent her voice to various commercials and narrative projects as a skilled voice artist.

Born with a heart that notices what others often overlook, Taamico has spent her life listening deeply—to people, to pain, to purpose. She carried the weight of unspoken truths early on, and now walks in the freedom of naming them—not to relive the past, but to reclaim it.

She is a woman who knows how to hold joy and sorrow in the same breath. A woman who believes healing doesn't always come loudly—but when it comes, it changes everything. Her work isn't performance. It's presence. It's legacy. It's love.

She resides in North Carolina and continues to create work that speaks to the soul—with intention, compassion, and truth.

Taamico Lahari, Author

taamicolahari.com

booking@taamicolahari.com

www.ingramcontent.com/pod-product-compliance
Lightning Source LLC
Chambersburg PA
CBHW031437120626
46545CB00006B/2444